An Management Briefing

ESOPs and the
Smaller Employer

M. Mark Lee, Editor

**A Division of
American Management Associations**

Library of Congress Cataloging in Publication Data
Main entry under title:

ESOPs and the smaller employer.

(An AMA management briefing)
  1. Employee ownership--Addresses, essays, lectures.
2. Corporations--Finance--Addresses, essays, lectures.
I. Lee, M. Mark, 1945-   II. Series: American
Management Associations. AMA management briefing.
HD5650.E17   658.32'25   79-23877
ISBN 0-8144-2244-6 (non-members)

©1979 AMACOM

A division of American Management Associations, New York.
All rights reserved. Printed in the United States of America.

*This Management Briefing has been distributed to all Limited
Company Members of the American Management Associations. A limited supply of extra copies is available at $5.00 a
copy for AMA members, $7.50 for nonmembers.*

First Printing

Contents

About the Authors

M. Mark Lee is a vice-president of Standard Research Consultants, a firm he joined in 1970. Vice-chairman of the valuation committee of the ESOP Association of America, Mr. Lee has prepared numerous studies for Standard Research Consultants, including valuations of restricted securities and ESOP feasibility studies, and prepared statistical studies for The New York Stock Exchange. He has also been a financial consultant to major U.S. industrial corporations on merger litigation and class actions.

A graduate of the Wharton School of Finance and Commerce of the University of Pennsylvania, Mr. Lee also holds an M.B.A. from the Graduate School of Business Administration of New York University. His articles have been published in business publications, including *Pension and Profit-Sharing Tax Journal* and *Financial Executive*.

Larry D. Blust is a tax partner with Jenner & Block in Chicago. Mr. Blust received a B.S. in accounting and a J.D. from the University of Illinois. He is a certified public accountant and a member of the American Bar Association. A regular lecturer on taxes for the Illinois Institute of Continuing Legal Education, Mr. Blust has also coauthored a number of books, including *Pension Practice* and *Business Acquisitions and Tender Offers.*

John E. Curtis, Jr., has served as counsel to the U.S. Senate Committee on Finance since 1977. He had primary staff responsibility for the committee's work in the areas of employee stock ownership plans, pension and profit-sharing plans, employee fringe benefits, and capital formation. Prior to his appointment to the committee staff, Mr. Curtis practiced law in Washington, D.C., and San Francisco, specializing in ESOPs and employee benefits. Mr. Curtis has written numerous articles, and lectures frequently on these topics. A graduate of Trinity College (B.A.) and the University of Virginia School of Law (J.D.), Mr. Curtis also holds a master of laws in taxation (L.L.M.) from Georgetown University Law Center.

John F. Tercek is an associate with Hirschfeld, Stern, Moyer & Ross, Inc. The firm renders actuarial, administrative, and consulting services in a broad area of employee benefits, and has been active in employee stock ownership plans since 1971. Mr. Tercek has been with HSM&R, Inc., since graduating from the Wharton School of Finance and Commerce at the University of Pennsylvania.

Introduction

WITH the passage of the Employee Retirement Income Security Act (ERISA) in 1974 and the Tax Reduction Act of 1975, ESOPs (employee stock ownership plans) and their Tax Act counterparts, TRASOPs, were touted as the way to instant wealth. Their adoption supposedly could almost automatically double the size of a corporation, increase profits geometrically, create instant employee happiness, and make private shareholders millionaires, without any cost to anyone except the Internal Revenue Service. Many companies adopted the concept wholeheartedly for real or imagined benefits. Others rejected it out of hand as another business fad.

Five years have now passed. Abuses have been uncovered and lawsuits have been instituted against some parties to ESOP transactions. As a result, much of the uninhibited enthusiasm for these employee benefit plans has waned despite the passage of additional favorable legislation by Congress. It is time for a quiet reappraisal of the application of the ESOP concept to the smaller corporation. ESOP is a valuable tool in the right business situation.

This briefing contains six related articles by Larry D. Blust, Esq., John F. Tercek, John E. Curtis, Jr., Esq., and myself on ESOP and its implementation and use. It was my privilege to work with three respected authorities, and I am grateful for the time and effort they devoted to this publication. I would also like to thank Norma Frankel and Rose Lockwood for helping edit this publication, and Michael S. Long, Sandra Greenhouse, and Helen V. Graney for typing it.

M. Mark Lee, Editor

7

1

ESOPs and How They Work

Larry D. Blust, Esq.

AN employee stock ownership plan (ESOP) is an employee benefit plan that invests primarily in employer securities. It has two purposes. The first is to encourage employees to own their employer's stock. The other is to aid in corporate financing. During the time an individual is an employee of the corporation, the stock acquired by an ESOP is held in a trust for him or her. The individual may or may not receive a pass through of voting rights and other rights of ownership. Generally, the stock is distributed by the trust only when the employee has terminated employment or died. Prior to 1979, most ESOPs had to distribute employer securities. However, the Revenue Act of 1978 eliminated this requirement for some plans. Cash may now be distributed to a participant or beneficiary of selected plans unless the participant requests otherwise. This right is likely to be extended to all ESOPs.

NONLEVERAGED ESOPs

Stock Bonus Plan

The basic type of ESOP, a stock bonus plan, has existed since 1939, when the provisions dealing with pension and profit-sharing plans were added to the Internal Revenue Code. A stock bonus plan is established and maintained by an employer to provide benefits similar to those of a profit-sharing plan except that:

1. Contributions to a stock bonus plan can be made by an employer even if the employer has no profits for the year involved. Thus, a stock bonus plan may be used to create a carryback or carryforward of a net operating loss.

2. Benefits from a nonleveraged stock bonus plan must be distributable in employer stock. The Internal Revenue Service has always interpreted this to mean that benefits must actually be distributed in employer stock. As noted above, the exception to this rule for some ESOPs is likely to be extended to all stock bonus plans.

In all other respects, stock bonus plans operate the same way profit-sharing plans do. The employer makes a contribution in either cash or employer securities to a trust whose trustees are appointed by the employer. The cash contributed, or the fair market value of the stock contributed, is deductible by the employer subject to certain limitations. Cash contributions to the trust must be invested by the trustee primarily in employer securities. The beneficiaries of the trust are the employees who meet certain nondiscriminatory standards. Contributions to a stock bonus plan are discretionary with the employer, but are limited to a maximum of 15 percent of covered compensation.

The amount of stock contributed to the trust or purchased with cash contributions is generally allocated to each plan participant in proportion to his or her compensation. The income, gains, and losses from investments are allocated to the participant's account in proportion to his or her account balances. After a number of years of service, a participant will be partially or fully vested in his or her account balance. Then, when he or she terminates employment, dies, or retires, employer securities equal to the account balance are distributed to the participant or his or her beneficiary. In order to be qualified employee benefit plans under the Internal Revenue Code, stock bonus plans must meet the same eligibility, vesting, reporting, disclosure, and other requirements of the Employees Retirement Income Security Act (ERISA) as profit-sharing plans.

For tax purposes, stock bonus plans have two uses that sometimes conflict. First, they constitute qualified employee benefit plans. Their use and desirability as such are discussed in greater detail in Section 2. As such plans, they have the following generally favorable tax advantages to employers and participants:

1. The employer may deduct contributions to the plan when made, but participants are not taxed on the contributions allocated

to them until the plan makes a distribution.

2. Even on a distribution, favorable estate or income tax treatment may be available to the participant or his beneficiary. On distribution, a participant is taxed only on the value of the shares when they were acquired by the trust. This amount is subject to the special ten-year averaging treatment, which will generally result in a rate of tax considerably lower than the participant's marginal tax rate on ordinary income. Any increase in value of the employer stock during the time it was held by the trust will be taxed at capital gains rates when the stock is sold by the participant.

3. The trust is tax exempt. Thus, dividends and other earnings can accumulate tax free. Consequently, employees participating in stock bonus plans can benefit from the compounding effect of investing dividends on a pretax basis.

Despite the advantages of stock bonus plans as qualified employee benefit plans, they did not catch on with closely held corporations until their second use, as a tax-sheltered capital-raising device, was emphasized to owners of closely held corporations. Employers' contributions of cash can be reinvested in the corporation immediately. Employers' contributions of stock to an ESOP create both a noncash charge and a tax deduction. This tax savings can be reinvested in the corporation.

Although the amount reinvested will generally be less than the proceeds from the sale of the same stock to an outside party, as a practical matter an ESOP contribution usually results in less dilution of control. While the stock is held in the trust, it is controlled by the ESOP's trustees, who are generally named and controlled by the corporation. Moreover, in a nonleveraged ESOP of a closely held corporation, there is no requirement that voting stock or even common stock is used. Even if voting stock is used, voting rights must be passed through to the participants only on corporate matters that require more than majority approval. Consequently, little or no dilution of control is necessary with a nonleveraged ESOP of a closely held corporation, while the stock is held by the trust.

However, as vested employees retire, terminate employment, or die, stock must be distributed from the ESOP trust to the participant or his beneficiary. In a closely held corporation, the non-ESOP shareholders may suffer dilution of control at this point if voting stock was used. Any dilution that occurs is likely to be temporary. Although employers with nonleveraged ESOPs are not required to give the participant a put to sell the stock back to the corporation, a closely held corporation—either by itself or through the ESOP—usually repurchases the stock shortly after it is distributed.

If the corporation repurchases the stock and retires it, there is a partial unwinding of its tax shelter; the corporation cannot deduct for tax purposes the cost of repurchasing the stock. If the ESOP repurchases the stock with a cash contribution by the corporation, or if the stock purchased by the corporation is recontributed to the ESOP, there is no unwinding of the shelter. Thus, distribution of the ESOP stock and its repurchase are generally not very painful so long as the corporation is growing and can make tax deductible contributions to the ESOP.

In addition to acting as a financing device, ESOPs have been proposed as a way to redeem the interests of existing shareholders in a closely held corporation. In this situation, an ESOP may act both as a means of financing a redemption and as a means of avoiding the rules treating certain redemptions as dividends. The entire amount of any distribution treated as a dividend is taxed as ordinary income to the seller at rates of up to 70 percent. If the redemption is not treated as a dividend, only the amount received in excess of tax cost (commonly called "basis") is taxed. This amount is generally taxable as a long-term capital gain, subject to a maximum rate of 28 percent.

Stock Bonus Plan Plus Money Purchase Pension Plan

Contributions to an ESOP that is either a profit-sharing or stock bonus plan are limited to 15 percent of covered compensation. ERISA allowed employers to increase this limit by using a money purchase pension plan designed to invest primarily in employer securities either in addition to or in lieu of a stock bonus or profit-sharing plan. The contribution to both plans (and all other qualified defined contribution plans) is then limited to 25 percent of covered compensation.[1] Money purchase pension plans, unlike profit-sharing and stock bonus plans, require a fixed contribution

---

[1]There is also a dollar limitation on contributions for each employee to all qualified contribution plans. This limitation started in 1974 at $25,000. Because of inflation, it had gone up to $32,700 in 1979.

formula. In the absence of compelling business necessity, the contribution required by the formula must be made to a money purchase pension plan each year, regardless of the employer's financial condition or need for financing. The pension plan, unlike a stock bonus plan, would not be required to distribute employer securities. In all other respects, it would operate in the same manner as a stock bonus plan.

LEVERAGED ESOPs (LESOPs)

ESOPs gained popularity in the late 1960s and early 1970s as leveraged financing devices. Assume, for example, that corporation X decided to have its ESOP trust borrow $500,000 instead of borrowing this money itself. The corporation could do this by guaranteeing the ESOP's loan, and by agreeing to make contributions to the ESOP sufficient to amortize both the principal and interest on the loan.

The ESOP would then borrow $500,000 and use this money to buy, say, 50,000 shares of stock from X. The corporation would use the money either to buy the assets it desired or as working capital, and the ESOP would pledge the stock as security for the loan. Each year X would make a tax-deductible contribution of $100,000, plus the interest on the loan, to the ESOP. The ESOP would use this amount to amortize the loan and would allocate one-fifth of the shares each year to the participants. The net effect would be that X would have paid only $250,000 in posttax dollars for the loan, and would have 50,000 more common shares outstanding. An ESOP that borrows money in this manner, on the security of the employer's guarantee, is commonly referred to as a leveraged ESOP, or LESOP.

There are a number of reasons a closely held corporation might use a LESOP rather than borrow money directly and shelter the repayment of principal through contributions to a nonleveraged ESOP. For example:

1. Current financing agreements may restrict additional borrowings but may not preclude the issuance of additional stock and a loan guarantee.

2. The LESOP may be used to purchase a large block of stock from a controlling shareholder or the relative of a controlling shareholder. If so, a direct purchase by the corporation may not be a feasible alternative, because of the constructive dividend risk

involved. If the purchase price exceeds the maximum annual contribution allowable to the ESOP, a LESOP may be necessary; an installment purchase would be considered a loan, and thus would be a prohibited transaction subjecting the selling shareholder to penalties if a nonleveraged ESOP were used.

LESOP Requirements

Prior to ERISA, many attorneys believed that LESOPs could not be used by closely held corporations because of the conflict of interest and problems of fiduciary responsibility discussed in Section 5. ERISA and subsequent legislation have largely eliminated these impediments. To control the risks to participants when the plan borrows money, Congress and the Internal Revenue Service have imposed various requirements on LESOPs. For this purpose, LESOPs are ESOPs that have either made, or are authorized to make, a loan from (or guaranteed by) a "disqualified person." Such loans are commonly referred to as "exempt loans." In general, employers, fiduciaries, officers, directors, highly compensated individuals, shareholders, and certain related parties are "disqualifed individuals."

Before 1979, a LESOP was subject to the following requirements (these did not apply to nonleveraged ESOPs):

1. The plan had to be a stock bonus plan or a combination stock bonus plan and money purchase pension plan. It could not be a money purchase pension plan standing alone or a profit-sharing plan.

2. The plan had to designate itself formally as an ESOP.

3. The LESOP could not be obligated to acquire securities from a particular security holder at an undetermined time, such as at a shareholder's death. It also could not be subject to any puts, other than the put described below that is required for leveraged stock.

4. The LESOP could not be integrated with Social Security.

5. The plan had to state specifically that it was designed to invest primarily in qualifying employer securities.

6. If a participant forfeited part of his account balance on termination, qualifying employer securities had to be forfeited last. If more than one class of such securities was allocated to a participant, a pro rata portion of each class had to be forfeited.

7. Valuation of securities had to be made in good faith based on all relevant factors. Valuation for purposes of transactions with dis-

qualified persons had to be made as of the date of the transaction. All other valuations had to be made as of the most recent valuation date under the plan. An independent appraisal by a person who customarily makes such appraisals was deemed a good faith determination of value, except with regard to transactions with disqualified persons.

8. If a loan was used to acquire more than one class of employer securities, a participant had to be allocated the same proportion of each class.

9. Exempt loans were subject to the following requirements:

(a) They had to be primarily for the benefit of the LESOP participants, not the employer or its shareholders.

(b) The interest rate had to be reasonable and could not be so high that plan assets might be dissipated.

(c) The terms of the loan had to be arm's length.

(d) The proceeds of the loan could be used only to acquire employer securities or to repay a prior exempt loan. A qualified employer security was limited to equity securities and marketable debt obligations.

(e) The debt could not have any recourse from the LESOP. The only assets of the LESOP that could be used as collateral were the employer securities acquired with the loan or the loan it repaid. Future contributions to the LESOP and earnings on the employer securities purchased with the loan could also be pledged as collateral.

(f) However, in the event of default, only collateral of sufficient value to pay the default could be forfeited. If the loan was directly from a disqualified party (rather than being guaranteed by a disqualified party), a default could not accelerate payments on the loan.

(g) Securities acquired with the exempt loan had to be placed in a suspense account and then allocated to participants' accounts and released as collateral for the loan as loan payments were made. The number of shares released and allocated had to be proportional to the principal and interest paid, unless special rules applied.

(h) The loan had to be for a specific term, but there was no limitation on this term or prepayment rights.

(i) Employer securities acquired by the LESOP with the exempt loan could be subject to a right of first refusal only if the right was in favor of either the LESOP or the employer, or both, and the stock was not publicly traded. The price and terms of this right had to equal the greater of those offered by a third party, or the LESOP valuation. The right of first refusal could exist only for 14 days after written notice of a third-party offer.

(j) If the employer security acquired with the loan was not publicly traded when distributed, the participant had to have the right (a "put") for fifteen months after the security was distributed to sell the security to the employer (or a substantial shareholder if it was known when the loan was made that the corporation would not be able legally to redeem the stock when it was distributed) at a price equal to the LESOP valuation. The payment period could not exceed five years without the consent of the participant.

Since the end of 1978, a LESOP has been subject to the following requirements in addition to those listed above:

1. Employer securities acquired by the LESOP with exempt loans must be either common stock readily tradeable on an established securities exchange or noncallable preferred, convertible into such common stock at a reasonable price. If the corporation does not have listed stock, the employer stock must have voting and dividend rights equal to or in excess of the employer's stock having the greatest voting power and the employer's stock having the greatest dividend rights. For this purpose, stock of another member of a controlled group must be considered. A 50 percent (or greater) owned subsidiary may use the stock of its parent or of another member of the controlled group.

2. The LESOP must pass through to participants the voting rights on publicly traded stock allocated to participants. On other stock voting rights must be passed through only for corporate matters requiring approval by more than a majority vote of the outstanding common stock voted.

3. A LESOP may distribute cash rather than shares unless the participant demands employer stock.

4. The put option on nontraded stock acquired with an exempt loan is modified. The participant or beneficiary may require the employer to purchase the stock at fair market value at any time up to six months after its receipt. After the close of the employer's taxable

year, the participant or beneficiary may require the employer to purchase it up to three months after notice of its valuation for plan purposes.

INVESTMENT CREDIT ESOPs (TRASOPs)

The leveraged ESOPs described above work by allowing an employer a tax deduction for its contribution. A deduction is only worth what the tax would have been on the amount deducted. Thus, for corporations with more than $100,000 in taxable income per year, a deduction for a one-dollar contribution to an ESOP generates only 46 cents more in available cash to the employer.

A credit against taxes generates a dollar-for-dollar reduction in taxes, since it directly offsets taxes that would otherwise be paid. Thus, a tax credit is over twice as valuable as a deduction to most employers. If an employer could get a tax credit for its contribution to a qualified retirement plan, the entire cost of the employee benefits under the plan would be funded by the federal government. The employer would incur no additional costs whatsoever by adding this fringe benefit. If a contribution of stock to an ESOP generated a tax credit equal to the stock's value, the employer would receive one dollar in cash, rather than 46 cents, for each dollar in stock contributed.

Tax credit for contributions to an ESOP first appeared in the Tax Reduction Act of 1975. ESOPs that generate a tax credit are commonly referred to as Tax Reduction Act Stock Ownership Plans or TRASOPs. An employer who establishes a TRASOP is allowed an additional 1 percent investment tax credit on new and used property, above the regular 10 percent investment tax credit, if the employer gives its own securities in an amount equal to the extra 1 percent credit to the TRASOP. Cash can also be contributed if it is used to purchase employer securities. The employer can get additional investment tax credit of up to ½ percent if participants in the TRASOP contribute an amount equal to the additional credit and the employer matches their contributions.

Since contributions to TRASOPs generate additional investment tax credits only to the extent that the employer has purchased property qualifying for the investment tax credit, TRASOPs work well only in capital-intensive industries. As discussed in Section 4, however, legislation to base the TRASOP credit on wages paid rather than qualified investment purchased is under consideration. If such legislation is passed, TRASOPs should be much more attractive to closely held corporations. Currently, the TRASOP rules expire at the end of 1983.

Requirements for TRASOPs

Since 1979, TRASOPs must be qualified retirement plans. Therefore, they must meet all requirements applicable, including those related to eligibility, participation, vesting, reporting, and disclosure. In addition, TRASOPs must meet the following requirements.

1. The plan must be designed to invest primarily in employer securities. Although TRASOP contributions must be invested entirely rather than primarily in employer securities to generate additional investment tax credit, a TRASOP feature can be added to an ESOP or LESOP so long as all the special rules described below are incorporated into the TRASOP portion of the plan.

2. TRASOP contributions must be made in employer securities or cash. Unlike a pension or profit-sharing plan, ESOP, or LESOP, contributions qualifying for the TRASOP credit may be made up to 30 days after the due date (including extensions) for the tax return of the current year (if the credit is to be taken in the current year or carried back to a prior year), or up to 30 days after the due date (including extensions) for a succeeding year to which the credit is to be carried over. Cash contributions must be invested in employer securities within 30 days.

3. The employer securities in which TRASOP contributions may invest are restricted to the same employer stock that may be purchased by LESOPs with exempt loans. The only difference is that *all* TRASOP contributions must be invested in such stock to qualify for the additional investment credit. There are two exceptions to this rule. Contributions can be used for the cost of establishing the TRASOP, if it does not exceed 10 percent of the first $100,000 contributed and 5 percent of the excess. The contributions can also be used to pay the cost of administering the plan up to 1 percent of the first $100,000 in dividends paid on TRASOP stock, plus 5 percent of the excess (but in no event more than $100,000).

4. TRASOP contributions are not deductible. They only qualify for the additional investment credit. If the property generating the credit is disposed of and the additional credit recaptured, the em-

ployer may then elect either to deduct the contribution recaptured or to apply it to reduce future TRASOP contributions. TRASOP contributions attributable to recaptured credits may no longer be withdrawn from the plan.

5. TRASOP stock must be allocated to all participants in proportion to their compensation, taking into account only the first $100,000 for each employee. The eligible participants are determined by the same rules applied to all qualified plans. Contributions to TRASOPs and LESOPs have the same maximums as other plans, except that the dollar limit referred to in footnote 1 above is doubled (or increased by the value of the contributed employer securities if this is less) if no more than one-third of the contributions for the year is allocated to officers, persons owning more than 10 percent of the stock each, or employees earning more than twice the regular dollar limitation. If this requirement is met, TRASOPs and LESOPs may be added to the employer's other qualified plans, rather than replacing such plans, if the employer is already providing maximum benefits. Allocations of TRASOP securities may be extended over such time as is necessary to meet the contribution allocation limits. Otherwise all TRASOP stock must be allocated immediately.

6. Each participant must have a nonforfeitable right to any TRASOP shares allocated to his account.

7. TRASOP stock cannot be distributed to a participant until 84 months after being allocated to his account unless the participant terminates employment, dies, or becomes disabled.

8. The same requirements on the pass through of voting rights apply to TRASOP stock as described above for LESOP stock.

9. TRASOPs must provide the same put options as LESOPs to sell to the employer any stock distributed to participants or beneficiaries.

10. A TRASOP, unlike other qualified retirement plans, may be established anytime prior to the employer's tax return due date (as extended) for the year in which the tax credit is claimed.

11. Contributions may only be withdrawn from TRASOPs that fail to qualify for Internal Revenue Service determination letters if the letter is applied for within 90 days after the ESOP credit is claimed, if approval of the plan is a condition of contribution, and if the contribution is returned within one year after notice that the plan does not qualify.

The additional investment tax credit is available if employees make their contributions anytime within two years after the employer's tax year in which the qualified investment is made. In order to qualify for this additional investment credit, the employee contributions to the TRASOP must be voluntary and the employer securities that are purchased with both the employee's contribution and the matching contribution must be allocated to the account of the employee making the contribution.

2

ESOPs as an Employee Benefit

John F. Tercek

EMPLOYEE stock ownership plans are now being used for such diverse purposes as creating a market for the orderly transfer of ownership in a closely held business, financing the divestiture of a subsidiary, and generating capital for expansion. Although attention has tended to concentrate on the ESOP's value as a corporate finance technique, many businessmen are attracted to its merit as an employee benefit. In this role, ESOP has a dual potential:

1. Future value as a supplemental retirement benefit that reflects the profitability and growth of the company during an employee's working years,

2. Immediate value to employees through the incentive provided by participation in company ownership.

In many companies, the effective combination of ESOP with other benefit programs may fulfill objectives of both the company and its employees. The objectives of employees and employers in the benefits area, and the types of plans devised to accommodate those objectives, have evolved and expanded throughout this century—especially in the past decade. Several factors have influenced this trend:

division to reduce overhead costs, and on a companywide basis, such as a Christmas bonus to all employees. Cash bonuses are treated as additional compensation—deductible by the employer and taxable to the employee. As continuing inflation pushes employees into higher income tax brackets, the after-tax income realized from cash bonus plans is diminishing. This is a major drawback to cash incentive plans.

The impact of high income tax rates on bonuses can be reduced if the bonus is deferred until retirement, when an employee should be in a lower tax bracket. Deferred bonus plans can be either qualified or nonqualified plans. Qualified deferred bonus plans are defined contribution plans such as profit-sharing plans and ESOPs, which meet the requirements of Section 401 of the Internal Revenue Code and the ERISA provisions. The primary tax advantage of qualified defined contribution plans is that employer contributions are deductible currently, but plan participants are not taxed until distribution.

In order to qualify for the tax advantages of qualified plans, IRS regulations mandate that the plans must benefit all employees and place limitations on the amount of current and deferred benefits accruing to highly paid employees. Employers who desire to provide additional benefits to a select group of executives must provide those benefits with "nonqualified" deferred compensation plans that are more stringently taxed. Employer contributions are not deductible until the employee-recipient is taxed.

Nonqualified plans can defer inclusion of a bonus in an employee's taxable income by deferring the employee's economic benefit and constructive (actual) receipt of the bonus. These plans often include "strings," such as requiring an employee to remain employed until retirement or to provide part-time consulting services after retirement. These clauses defer the economic benefit of the bonus by subjecting the bonus to future performance.

A nonqualified plan can defer the employee's constructive receipt of the bonus if the agreement is entered into before the compensation is earned and if the employer's promise is not secured in any way. Nonqualified deferred compensation plans often take the form of split-dollar life insurance plans, salary continuation plans, or tax-deferred annuities. Employers often utilize nonqualified plans to create incentives for management, and to attract and retain key executives.

The impact of high income tax rates on bonuses can be reduced further by investing the deferred bonuses in shares of stock of the employer corporation. Assuming a lump sum distribution, any future appreciation in the value of the stock will be taxed, when shares are sold after distribution, at the lower capital gains rate. Nonqualified bonus plans that attempt to reduce the employee's taxable income by turning it into capital gains include non-qualified stock bonus plans, stock option or purchase plans, and stock appreciation rights plans through which employees are invited to participate in any future growth in corporate value.

Plans of this nature are becoming less popular because they often require the employee to invest posttax dollars, or to pay current income tax on some part of the stock bonus, without giving him additional cash to pay the tax. In addition, IRS regulations are becoming increasingly restrictive in this area, and there is general uncertainty about future changes in taxation rules. Companies may continue to use nonqualified plans to reward select employees, but they are expanding the use of the tax-advantaged qualified plans to benefit all employees.

The ESOP is a qualified deferred bonus plan that reduces taxation of a participant's deferred bonus by investing primarily in shares of stock of the employer corporation and making distributions in shares of stock. Any appreciation in value over cost basis of employer stock in an ESOP distribution is taxed at the more favorable capital gains rate. In comparison, the profit-sharing type of qualified deferred bonus plan has traditionally invested in a diversified portfolio of marketable securities, corporate bonds, and insurance company mutual funds. No distinction is made between cost basis and appreciated value in a profit-sharing plan distribution.

Profit-sharing plans are permitted to invest in employer stock to the extent that such stock constitutes a prudent investment. The ESOP may offer additional incentives to employees because any growth in value of employer stock in each participant's account may be related more closely to his daily efforts than a typical profit-sharing plan, which invests in other companies. However, ESOP does not offer participants the same degree of financial security through investment diversification as a profit-sharing plan.

It should be noted that ownership of shares through an ESOP is not quite the same as outright ownership of shares. Employees have "beneficial" ownership of shares through ESOP, that is, ownership through participation in the plan. Employee participants share in any growth in corporate value, but shares in the ESOP trust are generally voted by the plan trustee at the direction of management.

The Revenue Act of 1978 included a provision to pass through voting rights in qualified plans that invest more than 10 percent of trust assets in employer stock that is not publicly traded. But this was required only on corporate issues that must be decided by more than a majority vote of outstanding common shares voted. Studies of the wisdom of this provision are currently being conducted by the Treasury Department, and these requirements are likely to be deleted in upcoming tax legislation.

There has been a marked trend toward investment in employer securities in qualified deferred bonus plans in the last decade. Poor performance and continued volatility in the stock market have prompted investment in company stock, where management and employees have greater control over stock performance. Many companies are combining an ESOP with a profit-sharing plan, which allows employers increased flexibility in planning contributions. Stock contributions can be made to the ESOP or cash contributions to the profit-sharing plan, depending on corporate cash flow. A combined ESOP/profit-sharing plan can benefit employees, also, by diversifying deferred bonuses into both a marketable securities portfolio and employer stock.

SPECIFIC CONSIDERATION OF AN ESOP

When a company is contemplating installing an ESOP, whether in combination with a profit-sharing plan, in conjunction with a pension plan, or as a sole qualified plan, specific areas should be considered. ESOP works well in labor-intensive companies with annual pretax profits in excess of $150,000 and prospects for continued profitability that will permit a full deduction of annual plan contributions from the new maximum corporate tax bracket. Steady growth in company (and share) value is ideal, as employees will feel that their efforts bring positive results. ESOP participant payroll should be over $400,000. ERISA limits annual ESOP contributions to 15 percent of covered compensation, or 25 percent of compensation when combined with a money purchase pension plan.

The setup costs for an ESOP can range from $10,000 to in excess of $100,000, depending on the complexity of the corporation and the plan and the degree of fiduciary exposure. Annual maintenance costs run from $5,000 to $30,000. It is unlikely that a corporation will want to incur fees of this magnitude if it is limited to an annual contribution of $50,000 or less.

Corporate owners should be ready philosophically to let employees own their stock. An ESOP's success in motivating employee participants depends in large part on the degree to which employees feel that they actually participate as owners. Employee communications should be designed to explain to employees both what ownership means in general and how they can affect the value of the shares they own through their individual and collective efforts. An effective employee communications program is an essential part of installing and maintaining a successful ESOP. It typically takes several years of ESOP contributions and communications before participants appreciate and respond to their new status as employee shareholders.

An ESOP can be a potential buyer for part or all of a major shareholder's shares. In this regard, the future of the company should not depend substantially on one man who intends to sell his entire interest. In other words, there should be some middle management who can and will grow to top managerial responsibilities, in order to maintain business profitability after an owner has transferred his interest.

After a company has installed an ESOP, the plan requires special attention on an ongoing basis. Like most post-ERISA qualified plans, an ESOP must be properly maintained and administered under the provisions of the Internal Revenue Code and ERISA. There are additional complexities in administering an ESOP compared with administering a pension or profit-sharing plan. These include keeping track of both the cost basis of each share of employer stock allocated to the account of each participant and the fair market value of each share.

If the ESOP is used as a financing device, further complexities arise, such as determining a nondiscriminatory method of allocating "suspended" or leveraged shares to participants' accounts. Employer stock of inactively traded companies that is acquired with the proceeds of an ESOP loan is subject to a put option to the employer when distributed to a participant. In any closely held company, the employer or the ESOP generally has an obligation to repurchase distributed shares. The future repurchase liability, which will increase as participants' accounts grow over the years, must be monitored to protect the company's future cash flow.

Also, there are possible conflicts between the interests of ESOP participants and those of the corporation. These conflicts and their legal implications are discussed more fully in Section 5. ESOP trustees should be aware of the problem that could arise with regard to holding company stock in the ESOP trust if the company is performing poorly. There can be an inherent conflict between the best interests of plan participants and those of the company in this situation, particularly if there is no outside market for the company's stock. Because a trustee must make decisions for the exclusive benefit of employees, it may be advisable to use an institutional ESOP trustee, with the counsel of an employee benefits attorney, rather than an officer of the company. Although special care must be exercised to comply with ESOP provisions under ERISA, they are not prohibitively restrictive.

ESOPs IN THE 1980s

Despite the complexity of employee stock ownership plans and the many considerations that must be evaluated prior to installing an ESOP, more companies every year are opening the door to employee participation in ownership through ESOPs. The most dramatic ESOP expansion has been in companies of 50 to 5,000 employees. Their total payrolls swollen by inflation, many of these medium-sized companies find that they now fit the ESOP criteria described above.

There are many factors behind the growth of ESOPs. Continued inflation erodes the future purchasing power of savings and level-benefit pension plans, and employees seek additional retirement benefits. In addition, employees today are looking for greater personal satisfaction from their jobs. Employers desire to increase worker productivity and seek new sources of investment capital.

The dual potential of ESOPs can help to achieve these objectives. ESOP can provide employees with a supplemental retirement benefit that reflects the financial fortunes of their company. Although a diversified securities portfolio may be a more conservative investment vehicle for supplemental retirement funds, employees may be attracted to the growth potential of a plan that invests in their own company. If properly communicated, each employee may appreciate how he can improve his own ESOP account by contributing to company growth and profitability.

Ideally, ESOP's potential as an employee incentive will lead to a greater cooperative effort between labor and management by establishing mutual goals of corporate success. Although it is difficult to trace changes in employee attitude or productivity to a specific source, some companies that have installed ESOPs have experienced lower absenteeisn, reduced employee theft, more employee suggestions, and a general improvement in attitude.

It appears that Congress will continue to encourage the concept of employee ownership. A proposed wage base tax credit for ESOPs is being considered to make employee stock ownership more attractive to corporate owners. Congress is also considering a Small Business Employee Stock Ownership Act, and an allowance for the deduction of ESOP installation and maintenance fees to make ESOP feasible for smaller companies. The new legislative proposals are discussed in Section 4. Many companies examined ESOP in the early 1970s and postponed greater involvement until regulatory uncertainty was resolved. Continued favorable legislation should encourage these and other companies to take another look at employee stock ownership plans in the 1980s.

3

ESOPs as a Technique of Corporate Finance

M. Mark Lee*

ESOPs (including TRASOPs and LESOPs) are primarily an employee benefit. Corporations and stockholders who attempt to use this concept only to further their own ends, at the expense of employees, must expect strong reactions from the Department of Labor and Internal Revenue Service, as well as from their employees. Nevertheless, these plans are designed to aid in corporate finance as well as to transfer ownership of the employer's stock to its employees.

The value of ESOPs in corporate finance has excited many potential users. Their attraction stems from the simple fact that, while employer contributions to an ESOP are deductible for both tax and financial accounting purposes, stock contributions do not withdraw any assets from the corporation, and cash contributions can either be reinvested in the corporation or be used by the ESOP to purchase stock (at capital gains rates to the seller) for distribution to employees. In this section, five facets of ESOPs as a technique of corporate finance are reviewed:

*Portions of Mr. Lee's articles have been adapted from material previously published in *Pension and Profit-Sharing Tax Journal* and in *Prentice-Halls Pension and Profit Sharing.*

1. The basic operation of an ESOP and its advantages and disadvantages compared with those of a cash contribution plan.
2. The advantages and disadvantages of using LESOPs and ESOPs in corporate financing.
3. The use of an ESOP to transfer ownership of corporate stock.
4. The advisability of using convertible preferred stock in an ESOP.
5. The financial impact of the put liability.

BASIC OPERATION AND IMPACT OF AN ESOP

Examples are the best way to understand the impact and operation of an ESOP. Table 1 presents the impact on a corporation of ESOP contributions that are either reinvested or used to purchase existing stock. The example assumes that the corporation has the following characteristics. First, it is capitalized by common stock only. Second, the return on a stockholder's investment in the corporation is 16 percent, both for existing stockholders' equity and for any new equity invested in the corporation. Third, 25 percent of earnings (with a minimum of 50 cents per share) are paid out as dividends, and 75 percent are retained in the corporation. Fourth, the fair market value of the stock is 7.25 times earnings, which is approximately equal to its book value per share. Fifth, earnings, dividends, and market price all increase at about the same compound growth rate—12 percent per year. Sixth, the covered payroll of the corporation increases at 6 percent per year. And seventh, the addition of an employee benefit plan yields no compensating increase in employee productivity.

The first column in Table 1 shows the corporation's profits, dividends, and investments in year 1 and year 5, assuming no additional employee benefit plan is adopted. The second column represents the same items for the first and fifth year, assuming that an additional employee benefit plan is adopted that requires a $200,000 investment at the end of the first year, with annual contributions increasing at 6 percent—the rate of growth of the covered payroll. The third and fourth columns show the operation of the corporation during the period, assuming that an ESOP is adopted instead of a cash contribution plan, and that either stock or cash is contributed to the ESOP.

32

During the first year, all three employer contributions reduced net posttax earnings by $100,000. The reduction is $100,000 instead of $200,000 because contributions are deductible for income tax purposes, and at a 50 percent tax rate they reduce income tax expense by $100,000. The cost of the contributions reduces earnings per weighted average share by ten cents. In addition, the cash contribution (either to the ESOP or to some other plan) reduces the potential stockholder's investment in the corporation by $100,000. In contrast, the $200,000 stock contribution to the ESOP (paid for by the $100,000 reduction in posttax earnings and the $100,000 reduction in income taxes) increases stockholders' investment by $100,000. This stock contribution also increases common stock outstanding by 29,000 shares.

By the end of year 5, assuming a compound return on stockholders' investment of 16 percent per year, the corporation's net earnings after taxes are $3,147,000 assuming no additional benefit plan; $3,119,000 assuming an ESOP plan with contributions made in stock; and $2,953,000 assuming cash contributions either to an ESOP or to some other benefit plan. The net earnings of the corporation are greatest when the corporation does not have any benefit plan because the costs of the plan are not deducted against earnings. Earnings are second highest with a stock contribution plan because, while the contribution is a deduction for both income tax and financial accounting purposes, operating earnings are greater due to the extra income from the tax savings reinvested in the corporation. Corporate earnings are the lowest with cash contributions both because these deductions are chargeable against the income of the corporation and because they are not reinvested in the corporation.

Earnings and dividends per share are highest when a corporation has no additional plan because there are no costs to bear and no additional shares of stock outstanding. The cash contributions (either to an ESOP or to some other plan) reduce earnings by approximately 20 cents per share. This is the cost to existing shareholders of adopting any cash contribution plan. This cost is the same whether cash contributions are used to buy defined benefits for employees or, by the ESOP to purchase employer stock from an external source.

The earnings per share of the employer are slightly higher if stock contributions are used rather than cash contributions, because the cost of contribution is fixed whether cash or stock is

Table 1. Impact on corporation of ESOP contributions either reinvested or used to purchase existing stock

		No Additional Plan	Cash Contribution Plan	ESOP Stock Contribution	ESOP Cash Contribution
Year 1					
Posttax operating earnings	($000)	2,000	2,000	2,000	2,000
Posttax cost of contribution	($000)	—	(100)	(100)	(100)
Net posttax earnings	($000)	2,000	1,900	1,900	1,900
Opening common equity	($000)	12,500	12,500	12,500	12,500
Dividend payment	($000)	(500)	(500)	(500)	(500)
Value of stock issued	($000)	—	—	200	—
Ending common equity including net posttax earnings	($000)	14,000	13,900	14,100	13,900
Earnings per weighted average share	($)	2.00	1.90	1.90	1.90
Dividends per weighted average share	($)	0.50	0.50	0.50	0.50
Shares outstanding					
Beginning of the year	(000)	1,000	1,000	1,000	1,000
End of the year	(000)	1,000	1,000	1,029	1,000

Year 5

Posttax operating earnings	($000)	3,147	3,079	3,245	3,079
Posttax costs of contribution	($000)	—	(126)	(126)	(126)
Net posttax earnings	($000)	3,147	2,953	3,119	2,953
Opening common equity	($000)	19,670	19,244	20,281	19,244
Dividend payment	($000)	(787)	(738)	(780)	(738)
Value of stock issued	($000)	—	—	252	—
Ending common equity including net posttax earnings	($000)	22,030	21,459	22,872	21,459
Earnings per weighted average share	($)	3.15	2.95	2.96	2.95
Dividends per weighted average share	($)	0.79	0.74	0.74	0.74
Shares outstanding	(000)				
Beginning of year		1,000	1,000	1,054	1,000
End of year	(000)	1,000	1,000	1,065	1,000

used, and there are more shares outstanding. Also, in this example it has been assumed that any new investments have the same earnings per share as prior investments in the corporation before the deduction of the contribution.

Whether earnings per share are reduced or increased by making stock contributions is a function of the profitability of the employer's new investments and the number of new shares issued. If new investments generate less earnings per share than existing investments, dilution will be increased because the total earnings of the corporation will not increase fast enough to keep up with the additional shares issued. If, on the other hand, the new investments generate earnings per share at a high enough rate, there will be no additional dilution through stock contributions, even when compared with not adopting any plan. However, with only a 50 percent tax savings, the return on the new investments of the corporation would have to exceed twice the return on its existing investments to prevent dilution.

Stock contributions dilute the ownership position of non-ESOP stockholders. In Table 1, non-ESOP stockholders own 100 percent of the corporation's outstanding stock if there is no contribution or if the contributions are in cash. If new stock is contributed to the ESOP, they own only 94 percent of the corporation (1,000,000/1,-065,000).

TYPES OF FINANCING

Table 2 shows three types of corporate financing: loan financing, stock bonus plan and loan financing, and leveraged ESOP financing. This table was prepared on the same basis as Table 1, with the additional assumption that the corporation has taken out a ten-year $2,640,000 loan, amortized at the annual rate of stock contributions made by the corporation over a ten-year period.

A stock bonus plan combined with a loan differs from a leveraged ESOP. Under a stock bonus plan, the ESOP receives annual stock contributions equal in value to the annual principal payments on the loan. The loan is a direct obligation of the corporation. Although the payments on the principal of the loan are not tax deductible, the stock contributions each year are deductible and reduce corporate income taxes.

Under the typical leveraged ESOP, the employees' stock plan borrows funds with which to purchase new employer stock immediately. The employer corporation guarantees this loan and promises to make large enough annual contributions to the plan to meet the interest costs and amortization payments of the loan. These annual contributions to the LESOP are tax deductible. All shares to be issued under a LESOP financing plan are issued at the beginning of the financing transaction.

Table 2 illustrates that on a per-share basis, loan financing results in the highest earnings and dividends. The second-best method is the stock bonus plan combined with loan financing, and the worst method is the LESOP. The loan financing method has the advantage of increasing earnings without increasing either employee benefit contributions or the number of shares outstanding. The stock bonus plan and loan combination has the advantage over the LESOP of issuing fewer shares of stock, since it is assumed that there will be an annual increase in the fair market value of the common stock outstanding. Because the principal payments are fixed under both methods, as the stock price rises, fewer shares are issued under the combination method.

The stock bonus plan and leveraged ESOP have one significant advantage over the loan financing method—they both create larger corporations, in terms of total income and common equity. Under the loan financing method there are no contributions of stock creating tax savings that can be reinvested in the corporation.

TYPES OF STOCK ISSUED

Convertible preferred stock can be contributed to some employee stock ownership plans under ERISA. Contributing this kind of stock instead of common stock has two advantages. First, assuming that preferred stock is convertible at a price higher than the fair market value of the corporation's common stock, fewer voting common shares will be outstanding even after conversion of the preferred stock. Second, the convertible preferred stock can provide the ESOP, or a participating employee, with a regular income. Although at the present time this dividend income is not tax deductible, dividends paid to an ESOP may become tax deductible in the future.

Table 2. Impact of comparative financing plans

		Loan Only	Loan and Stock Bonus Plan	Leveraged ESOP
Year 1				
Posttax operating earnings	($000)	2,422	2,422	2,422
Posttax interest expense	($000)	(106)	(106)	—
Posttax value of contribution	($000)	—	(100)	(206)
Net posttax earnings	($000)	2,316	2,216	2,216
Debt payment	($000)	200	200	200
Debt balance—year-end	($000)	2,440	2,440	2,400
Opening common equity	($000)	12,500	12,500	12,500
Dividend payment	($000)	(579)	(554)	(602)
Stock issued or freed	($000)	—	200	200
Ending common equity(a)	($000)	14,237	14,362	14,314
Total invested capital(b)	($000)	16,677	16,802	16,754
Earnings per weighted average share	($)	2.32	2.22	1.84
Dividends per weighted average share	($)	0.58	0.55	0.50
Shares outstanding				
Beginning of year	(000)	1,000	1,000	1,203
End of year	(000)	1,000	1,012	1,203

Year 5

Posttax operating earnings	($000)	3,592	3,695	3,684
Posttax interest expense	($000)	(71)	(71)	—
Posttax value of contribution	($000)	—	(126)	(197)
Net posttax earnings	($000)	3,521	3,498	3,487
Debt payment	($000)	252	252	252
Debt balance—year-end	($000)	1,514	1,514	1,514
Opening common equity	($000)	20,681	21,329	21,260
Dividend payment	($000)	(880)	(875)	(872)
Stock issued or freed	($000)	—	252	252
Ending common equity(a)	($000)	23,322	24,204	24,127
Total invested capital(b)	($000)	24,836	25,718	25,641
Earnings per weighted average share	($)	3.52	3.34	2.90
Dividends per weighted average share	($)	0.88	0.84	0.72
Shares outstanding				
Beginning of year	(000)	1,000	1,046	1,203
End of year	(000)	1,000	1,056	1,203

(a)Includes net posttax earnings.
(b)Includes debt outstanding and stockholders' equity at year end.

Table 3. Impact of Issuing Common Stock

		Common Stock Contribution	Preferred Stock Contribution
Year 1			
Posttax operating earnings	($000)	2,000	2,000
Posttax value of contribution	($000)	(100)	(100)
Net posttax earnings	($000)	1,900	1,900
Preferred dividends	($000)	—	—
Earnings available for common stock	($000)	1,900	1,900
Preferred stock outstanding	($000)	—	200
Opening common equity	($000)	12,500	12,500
Dividend payment	($000)	(500)	(500)
Value of stock issued	($000)	200	—
Ending common stock-holders' equity[a]	($000)	14,100	13,900
Total stockholders' equity	($000)	14,100	14,100
Earnings per weighted average share	($)	1.90	1.90
Dividends per weighted average share	($)	0.50	0.50
Common shares outstanding year-end	(000)	1,000	1,000
Convertible preferred shares outstanding year-end	(000)	—	2

[a]Includes earnings available for common stockholders.

Table 3 presents the operation of an ESOP under the same assumptions made for Table 1, with the exception that in the second column of Table 3 it is assumed that convertible preferred stock, rather than common stock, is contributed to the ESOP. The preferred stock has a par value of $100 with a $10 coupon and is convertible into three shares of common stock.

Data are shown for the first and tenth year of the plan. As shown in this table, common stock earnings and dividends are slightly higher when preferred stock is issued to the ESOP rather than common stock, even assuming conversion of the preferred shares. However, the comparison also shows that the preferred dividend

Versus Convertible Preferred Stock

		Common Stock Contribution	Preferred Stock Contribution
Year 10			
Posttax operating earnings	($000)	5,897	5,767
Posttax value of contribution	($000)	(170)	(170)
Net posttax earnings	($000)	5,727	5,597
Preferred dividends	($000)	—	215
Earnings available for common stock	($000)	5,727	5,382
Preferred stock outstanding	($000)	—	2,640
Opening common equity	($000)	36,858	33,746
Dividend payment	($000)	(1,432)	(1,346)
Value of stock issued	($000)	340	—
Ending common stockholders' equity[a]	($000)	41,493	37,782
Total stockholders' equity	($000)	41,493	40,422
Earnings per weighted average share	($)	5.17	5.26
Dividends per weighted average share	($)	1.29	1.35
Common shares outstanding year-end	(000)	1,107	1,000
Preferred shares outstanding year-end	(000)	1,116	24

reduces the earnings that can be reinvested in the corporation. Thus, a corporation that contributes preferred stock has smaller total earnings and invested capital than one that contributes only common stock.

STOCK REPURCHASES

Either a corporation or its ESOP can purchase stock from existing shareholders. Generally, it is more advantageous to the shareholder to have the ESOP make the purchase because profits from

Table 4. Impact of Stock Purchases

		No Purchase	ESOP Purchase	Corporate Redemption
Year 1				
Posttax operating earnings	($000)	2,000	2,000	2,000
Posttax contribution	($000)	—	500	—
Net posttax earnings	($000)	2,000	1,500	2,000
Opening common equity	($000)	12,500	12,500	12,500
Dividend payment	($000)	(500)	(500)	(500)
Redemption	($000)	—	—	(1,000)
Ending common equity	($000)	14,000	13,500	13,000
Earnings per weighted average share	($)	2.00	1.50	2.00
Dividends per weighted average share	($)	0.50	0.50	0.50
Shares outstanding				
Beginning of year	(000)	1,000	1,000	1,000
End of year	(000)	1,000	1,000	929
Year 2				
Net posttax earnings	($000)	2,240	2,160	2,080
Opening common equity	($000)	14,000	13,500	13,000
Dividend payment	($000)	(560)	(540)	(520)
Ending common equity	($000)	15,680	15,120	14,560
Earnings per share	($)	2.24	2.16	2.24
Dividends per share	($)	0.56	0.54	0.56
Shares outstanding	(000)	1,000	1,000	929

the transaction are then taxable at capital gains rates. If the corporation makes the purchase, the seller's profit may be taxable at ordinary income rates.

The impact on the corporation of having the ESOP purchase on existing stockholder's stock, compared with having the corporation redeem the stock, is shown in Table 4. The same assumptions are used in this table as are used in Table 1, except that it is assumed that 71,000 common shares, worth $1 million, are purchased at the end of year 1. The ESOP purchase is made with a $1 million cash contribution from the corporation.

When the ESOP makes the purchase, the earnings of the corporation are reduced by $500,000, or 50 cents per share. Common stockholders' equity is also reduced by $500,000. Earnings are not reduced when the corporation makes the redemption, but stockholders' equity is reduced by $1 million, and common shares outstanding are reduced by 71,000 shares.

In year 2, the net posttax earnings of the corporation are $80,000 greater if the ESOP makes the purchase than if the corporation redeems the stock directly, because earnings on the extra $500,000 remain in the corporation ($500,000 times 16 percent).

Although the ESOP purchase increases the earnings of the corporation in the second year, the increased amount does not match the net posttax earnings when no redemption is made. As the ESOP purchase does not reduce the number of shares outstanding, earnings and dividends per share are reduced. The corporate redemption reduces the earnings of the corporation and the number of shares outstanding in proportion, with the result that the corporation's earnings and dividends per share are not reduced. While the corporation as a whole is better off with an ESOP purchase, stockholders who do not have their shares redeemed have reduced earnings and dividends.

THE PUT LIABILITY

After several years of operation, a closely held corporation and its ESOP may be faced with the obligation to redeem shares that have been distributed to employees. The number of shares to be redeemed in any given year is a function of the past contributions of stock to the ESOP, the turnover rate of participants, the vesting schedule, and the age of the participants. Redemptions made by the employer are not tax deductible. However, redeemed shares can be recontributed to the ESOP, in order to receive a tax deduction and to maintain the plan. The net effect would be similar to a cash contribution, as long as the corporation is not faced with the necessity of redeeming stock with a greater value than the maximum ESOP contribution permitted in any given year. This may not be the case when:

1. The fair market value of the corporation's stock consistently rises faster than its covered payroll.

2. A redemption of stock required in any given year is substantially higher than the maximum permitted contribution to the ESOP in that year.

3. The ESOP is terminated.

It is usually possible to anticipate redemptions in excess of the maximum permitted ESOP contribution, and to plan for them. For example, ESOP contributions can be reduced in some years, cash contributions can be made to the ESOP and compounded at tax-free rates, and extended payment terms can be built into the plan.

CONCLUSION

ESOPs are best viewed as employee benefit plans that can aid in corporate finance. Their advantage to the employer lies in its ability to retain a portion of its contribution for reinvestment. Their advantage to existing shareholders is the ability to sell their stock at capital gains rates. Assuming that a corporation can generate an adequate return on new investments, stock contributions to an ESOP will be less costly than the adoption of any cash contribution plan. In addition, stock contributions will increase the total earnings and equity in a corporation. However, unless a corporation has the opportunity to invest at very high rates of return, stock contributions to an ESOP will result in dilution of both ownership and earnings per share if the alternative is to adopt no additional plan.

Borrowing through an ESOP, either by combining an ESOP with a loan or using a LESOP, makes sense if a corporation is interested in establishing an additional employee benefit plan and is concerned about building the total shareholders' equity and earnings of the

These closings often followed a determination by the parent corporation that a subsidiary was simply not as profitable as other business operations of the corporate group. Sometimes such closings followed the death of the owner of the company. As these businesses closed, jobs were lost, local unemployment increased, and the tax base on which the community functioned was reduced. Members of Congress recognized the need to develop a way to maintain these businesses in their present locations.

In addition, Senators Long and Nelson, along with Sen. Donald Stewart and Sen. Mike Gravel, questioned whether the U.S. Congress should bail out such businesses and channel the profits back into the pockets of a limited number of shareholders. They argued that the employees should be given a stake in the future of these companies as well. For this reason, the thrust of the bill is to provide loan guarantees, through the Economic Development Administration of the Department of Commerce, for employee groups or employee-community groups to acquire ownership of these companies.

The bill specifically states that one way employees can acquire ownership of the company is through an ESOP. Although an ESOP is not the only ownership vehicle the bill permits, it clearly is the one that provides the most significant tax advantages for the new owners acquiring the company. Accordingly, it is anticipated that a majority of the employee groups that acquire ownership of companies under this act will do so through an ESOP.

Under this legislation, if a plant or a company is threatened with closing, the employees or an employee-community group would be eligible for Economic Development Administration loan guarantees. The EDA is empowered under the act to guarantee up to 75 percent of the total amount being borrowed by the new ownership group. Local financial institutions are expected to lend the other 25 percent of the necessary funds without the security of the federal loan guarantee. This is intended to assure that local lending institutions do, indeed, feel that the business is viable.

At this time it is unclear how much funding will be given to EDA for this program. But with the entire EDA appropriation due this year, a significant portion of that funding is expected to be channeled into this program. On May 1, 1979, the EDA advised Sen. William Proxmire, chairman of the Senate Committee on Banking and Urban Affairs, of its continued support for employee stock ownership plans.

EMPLOYER STOCK OWNERSHIP IMPROVEMENTS ACT OF 1979

The major thrust into the area of employee stock ownership in 1979 is in the tax incentives Congress is providing. Many of the provisions contained in the Employee Stock Ownership Improvements Act of 1979 (S. 1240) were initially contained in S. 3241, the Expanded Employee Stock Ownership Act of 1978. For example, in S. 3241, Congress considered for the first time the concept of providing a tax credit (similar to the investment tax credit first made available to tax credit ESOPs under the Tax Reduction Act of 1975) for labor-intensive companies. Although that provision was not enacted into law in 1978, the idea has gained significant support.

On Oct. 3, 1978, the Treasury Department sent all senators an analysis of each provision of the Revenue Act of 1978. In analyzing the provisions on ESOPs, the Treasury Department stated that "we do believe that the investment credit base for TRASOPs should be converted to a partial credit based on wages." In addition, on Sept. 22, 1978, Stuart Eizenstat, assistant to the president for domestic affairs and policy, wrote to Senator Long on ESOPs. In that letter, Mr. Eizenstat stated that "the challenge is to move toward broadened stock ownership in a way which is . . . fair both as between different industries and firms and employees within a given business enterprise." Clearly, this is directed toward a payroll-based tax credit, which would provide an equal benefit to each employee-participant. Finally, at the conclusion of the Senate debate on H.R. 13411 (Oct. 10, 1978), Sen. Jacob Javits, who has been critical of ESOPs in the past, made the following statement regarding employee stock ownership: "If a tax credit is to be provided for TRASOPs, I would prefer using a wage base for such a credit rather than an investment base." These statements all reflect a common feeling about the wage-based tax credit.

The labor-based tax credit is set forth in Section 3 of the 1979 bill; in addition, in Section 2 of that bill Congress makes the investment tax credit for plan contributions permanent. If these legislative initiatives are enacted, an employer will have the option of electing either credit in a particular year. The legislation also makes it clear that the employer may elect to claim only a portion of the credit in any year.

Other provisions contained in S. 3241—which are also part of the new legislation—include the tax deduction available to corporations declaring a dividend on stock held by ESOPs (or tax-credit

ESOPs) and passing those dividends through the plan to participants. The estate tax exclusion will also be available to anyone who, by gift or bequest, leaves stock in his company to an ESOP or tax-credit ESOP.

To be sure, the dividend deduction will affect revenue; however, that impact is not great compared with many of the tax proposals presented to and enacted by Congress each year. More importantly, the estate tax exclusion should eventually increase revenue, because amounts that are currently left to charities are forever lost to the federal revenue system when they become the property of tax-exempt charities. Bequests to an ESOP or a tax-credit ESOP keep these monies within the system of federal taxation. Because these bequests will eventually be distributed to participants in the plans, they will be taxable and again become a part of the free-enterprise system.

In order to encourage small employers to provide stock ownership for their employees, and recognizing that ESOPs have traditionally been more expensive to set up than other employee benefit plans, the bill also provides a tax credit of up to $5,000 of the small business employer's cost toward establishing such a plan. A small business employer is defined in the bill as one with no more than 100 employees.

Under section 415 of the Code, in determining the maximum amount that can be allocated to a participant's account under an ESOP or other employee benefit plan, all employer contributions, forfeitures, and a portion of employee contributions must be taken into account. This creates a problem for an employer that leverages through an ESOP. The employer contribution must be made each year to permit the ESOP to amortize its indebtedness; yet unexpected employee turnover could produce such a large forfeiture reallocation in a particular year that the section 415 limitations would be exceeded. In such a case, the plan could be disqualified. Accordingly, the bill excludes from computation under section 415 any extraordinary forfeiture allocation amounts that, when combined with the employer contributions necessary to amortize the ESOP's indebtedness, would exceed the limitation of section 415.

Certain employers, such as magazine publishers and publishers of independent newspapers, have traditionally been concerned about having competitors acquire inside information about their business operations. As a consequence, they restrict ownership of stock in the company. This has made ESOPs unattractive to them, since in the past stock has been distributed from these plans to people who no longer work for the company.

In an effort to encourage these employers to provide broader stock ownership within the company, the bill provides a greater protection. If an employer's by-laws or corporate charter restricts stock ownership to actual employees or qualified employee trusts, the bill permits the ESOP or the tax-credit ESOP to distribute a terminated participant's vested benefit in cash only, irrespective of the provisions of Code Section 409A(h).

In looking at distributions of stock from ESOPs and tax-credit ESOPs, Congress recognized that the current law regarding immediate taxation of these distributions was creating a problem for terminated participants who elected to receive distributions of employer stock. In essence, these people were expressing a desire to remain stockholders in their former company. However, since amounts distributed from the plan were subject to taxation in the year of distribution, distributees were frequently forced to sell the stock in order to pay the taxes.

To rectify this problem, it was determined that a certain amount of such stock distribution should not be taxable until the stock was actually sold. The main issue was what dollar limitation (or other restrictions) to put on such an exemption, since federal tax revenues are being deferred as well. In an effort to accommodate these competing interests, the bill provides a tax exemption only for the first $5,000 of such an ESOP distribution. In addition, the individual must have been a participant in the plan for at least three years prior to the distribution. Any determination of whether to extend this exemption to ESOPs, or to increase the dollar limitation, will depend on the effects of the present provision.

The bill also tries to resolve a problem that has existed for employees who participate in a tax-credit ESOP to the exclusion of any other qualified plan. ERISA specifically precludes the establishment of an individual retirement account (IRA) by any employee who is an active participant in a qualified plan. Since the employee's benefit under a tax-credit ESOP would generally be much smaller than what an employee could contribute to an IRA, many employees felt that they were being unfairly treated. They had to elect to acquire an ownership in employer stock or have the IRA. Also, many employers were concerned about permitting employees to elect not to participate in the plan, since it could result in failure to satisfy the requirements of Section 410 of the IRS Code. Accordingly, in an effort to resolve this conflict, the bill would allow an employee who participates only in a tax-credit ESOP to establish and contribute to an IRA as well.

A major impediment to claiming the additional ½ percent investment tax credit created by the Tax Reform Act of 1976 has been the requirement that employees make contributions to match the ½ percent amount. Due to a lack of regulation from the IRS and the Treasury Department and a great deal of confusion about the whole issue, most employers have elected to forego this additional credit. The Treasury Department has also become concerned that only more highly compensated employees actually contribute; lower paid employees are unable to make meaningful contributions, and the additional ½ percent in employer contributions are therefore allocated to higher paid groups.

To resolve these problem areas, the bill permits the employer to make matching contributions on behalf of its employees. In effect, the employer would receive the full 1½ percent investment tax credit provided by the Code, and a ½ percent tax deduction for the contribution on behalf of employees. To allay the concern of the Treasury Department that discrimination exists, the bill requires that each participating employee receive an allocation of this additional amount.

The bill also contains the ESOP changes set forth in the 1979 Technical Corrections Act. The most important of these are setting workable effective dates for the Revenue Act of 1978, establishing names for such plans, and redefining requirements for employer securities and qualifying employer securities.

Finally, the bill revises the provisions contained in the 1978 act regarding the pass through of voting rights to participants. This revision is most important for employers with closely held stock. By deleting section 401(a)(22) of the Code, the bill removes the pass through of voting rights for ESOPs, profit-sharing plans, stock bonus plans, and money purchase plans that invest more than 10 percent of their assets in closely held employer securities (or qualifying employer securities).

Assuming that this legislation is enacted, where will the issue of the pass through of voting rights stand? For publicly traded companies that establish a tax-credit ESOP or an ESOP, there is a complete pass through of voting rights to plan participants on all corporate issues. For closely held companies that establish a tax-credit ESOP, there is a mandatory pass through on issues that, by state law or corporate charter, require *more* than a majority vote. Traditionally, these issues would be of the caliber of mergers, acquisitions, or disposition of substantially all the corporation's assets.

For a closely held company that establishes an ESOP or any other defined contribution plan, regardless of the amount of plan assets invested in stock of the employer, there will be no mandatory pass through of voting rights to plan participants on any corporate issue. In addition, recognizing that there may be valid reasons for the use of nonvoting stock by an employer, the bill would permit the use of nonvoting employer securities (or qualifying employer securities) in a tax-credit ESOP or ESOP, provided that the stock is acquired from an individual other than the employer and that the individual owned the stock for two years. If the seller acquired the stock from somebody else (again, not the employer), together they must have owned it for at least two years.

LEGISLATIVE OUTLOOK

What is the prognosis for the legislation introduced in 1979? The answer is related to the types of incentives being created by the legislation. Historically, since Senator Long has been the major force behind employee stock ownership legislation in Congress, most of the legislative initiatives have been tax-oriented. This has acted as an immediate inducement for employers to provide stock ownership for their employees; however, because tax incentives have a negative impact on the federal budget, these legislative initiatives are always harder to enact. This is especially true in the political climate of 1979 and 1980, when people are concerned about spiraling inflation and "balancing" the federal budget.

It would seem that the technical, nonrevenue aspects of the Employee Stock Ownership Improvement Act of 1979 should be passed by Congress during 1979 and 1980. Certainly any changes contained in the 1979 Technical Corrections Act should pass, since the technical nature of nonrevenue aspects of those changes has already been agreed upon by the Treasury Department. Changes contained in this bill that have only a minor impact on the federal budget also seen likely to pass.

However, the major question is the future of those items (the labor-based tax credit, the permanency of the 1½ percent investment tax credit, and the tax credit for small employers who establish employee stock ownership plans) that do have a major budgetary impact. As explained at the outset, a great deal of support exists in the Administration for the labor-based tax credit, if the budget can support it. The projections made last fall by the Treasury Department and the staff of the Joint Committee on Taxation were quite high, as high as $1.9 billion. This provision, like other tax-credit incentives, can only be enacted if it has the direct support of the business community.

For the other bills that have been introduced, the Small Business Employee Ownership Act and the Voluntary Broadened Stock Ownership, Job Preservation, and Community Stabilization Act, the prognosis is clearly brighter since there are no tax incentives being created and therefore there is no revenue loss. The Small Business Employee Ownership Act was attached by amendment to S.918, an authorization bill for the Small Business Administration, and was passed by a House–Senate conference before Congress adjourned for the August 1979 recess. The bill was expected to be sent to the president in early September.

The House version of the Voluntary Broadened Stock Ownership, Job Preservation, and Community Stabilization Act was reported out by the House Banking Committee by May 1 and sent to the House for a vote; its Senate counterpart was attached by amendment to S.914, the National Public Works and Economic Development Act of 1979. The Senate bill passed the Senate in late July. The House bill was expected to pass in September, with a House–Senate conference expected to take up these bills, integrate them, pass the final version, and sent it to the president by late September.

5

Legal Problems of ESOPs

Larry D. Blust, Esq.

DESPITE the advantages of ESOPs as benefit plans and financing devices for closely held corporations, relatively few employers currently maintain ESOPs. The legal status of ESOPs in the past was unclear, and the risks for a plan investing in a closely held corporation, or borrowing money, were great. Most attorneys and advisors either did not suggest ESOPs, or advised against their use.

Despite the recent legislation, there are still some legal and practical problems. Consequently, ESOPs will not work for every closely held business that may want to use them to aid in financing. A knowledge of the problems, and possible solutions, in four areas—fiduciary responsibility, leveraging, dilution, and securities laws—is necessary when considering an ESOP.

FIDUCIARY RESPONSIBILITY

Prudence of Investment

ESOPs are trusts. A trustee is a fiduciary to the beneficaries of the trust, and thus has certain responsibilities both under state trust law and under ERISA. Generally, a trustee must invest trust assets in the same manner a prudent man would invest his own assets.

Investment in the stock of a closely held corporation is often not prudent. A minority interest in a closely held corporation is generally not marketable. The only potential buyers for such stock are, as a rule, the corporation or its controlling shareholders. Moreover, many closely held corporations are severely underfinanced. This is particularly true of the corporations to which ESOPs are most attractive—those with problems raising capital. In addition, the survival of many closely held corporations depends on the survival and business abilities of their controlling shareholders.

It is questionable whether the regular standard of prudence would be applied to an ESOP containing a provision requiring investment in employer securities. The legislative history of ERISA indicates that the prudent man standard is to be interpreted in harmony with the special nature and purposes of the plan involved. For example, the normal requirement of trust diversification is waived.

Although a lesser standard is likely to be applied to ESOPs, there is some point at which it becomes imprudent even for an ESOP to invest in employer securities. For example, if the corporation cannot reasonably be expected to survive for more than a short time, an investment in employer stock would appear imprudent. Even if the trustee is not responsible for the imprudent investment due to the plan requirement, the employer probably would be by having adopted such a plan. Thus ESOPs should not be used when the employer's financial survival is questionable, or in a personal services business if the corporation is not likely to survive the death of its founder or controlling shareholders.

The prudence of investment standard applies to continuing investments as well as the initial investment. This problem is not eliminated by the employer contributing securities to the ESOP rather than cash. When securities are contributed, the trustees may have a duty to question their valuation, and to attempt to sell them at whatever price can be realized.

Self-Dealing and Prohibited Transactions—The Need for Valuation

Trustees are generally prohibited from dealing with the trust. When allowed, such transactions are closely scrutinized. In an ESOP, the trustee is usually appointed by and serves at the pleasure of the employer. In a closely held corporation, corporate trustees may be reluctant to serve as ESOP trustees because plan assets are invested in nontraded securities, and they are potentially liable under the standard of prudence. Thus, the trustees of an ESOP are often the employer's officers or controlling shareholders. Their interests may conflict with the interests of the ESOP participants.

For the above reasons, there have been rules for many years either prohibiting or limiting transactions between qualified plans and employers (or officers, directors, or more than 10 percent shareholders of employers). The employer and such individuals are referred to as "disqualified persons" or "parties in interest." Most transactions with disqualified persons are "prohibited transactions" under ERISA, resulting in penalty taxes on the parties involved.

In a closely held corporation, the ESOP usually must buy employer stock from a disqualified person, since stock is only available from the corporation or its controlling shareholders. As one might expect, there is an exemption from the prohibited transaction rules that allows an ESOP to purchase employer stock from a disqualified person, provided the price is fair and determined on an arm's-length basis and no sales commission is incurred.

Thus, the ability of an ESOP to purchase employer stock is conditional on the payment of the fair market value of the stock. If employer stock is purchased for more than fair market value from a disqualified person, the purchase constitutes a prohibited transaction. The seller is liable for an initial 5 percent per year nondeductible excise tax on the value of the consideration received, plus an additional excise tax equal to 100 percent of such consideration unless the transaction is corrected within 90 days after notice. Any plan fiduciary who engages in such a transaction may be held personally responsible for any resulting losses to the ESOP.

Thus it is crucial that all the ESOP's purchases of employer stock be at fair market value. When there is a generally recognized independent market for the employer stock involved, the prevailing market price on the date of the transaction must be used in determining fair market value. When there is no generally recognized market, the fair market value must be determined in good faith by the ESOP trustee. It is prudent, although not essential, for ESOP trustees to seek an independent professional appraisal before entering into a purchase of stock from the employer or some other disqualified person.[1]

Valuation of closely held stock is very difficult. Because of these difficulties and the necessity of a good faith valuation, this problem is discussed separately in Section 6.

Prudence of Borrowing

The prudence standard discussed above relates to the trustee's judgment in borrowing money as well as in investing in employer securities. As a practical matter, there is no real prudence problem in most cases. The rules for exempt loans, as discussed in Section 1, are aimed at minimizing the risk of such loans to ESOP participants. Moreover, it is clear that Congress intended LESOPS to be used as leveraged financing devices. The prudence is likely to be applied in light of the purpose of the LESOP, and is only likely to be a problem in extreme cases of abuse.

Prohibited Transactions and Exempt Loans

The prohibited transaction rules apply to indirect as well as direct loans. An employer guarantee of a loan to an ESOP is a prohibited transaction unless the loan is exempt. As a result, an ESOP borrowing money on the strength of a guarantee or other collateral provided by the employer (or employee, officer, director, or 10 percent shareholder) must meet the special requirements explained in Section 1 for LESOPs. The loan itself must be an exempt loan.

The primary benefit requirement of exempt loans is likely to be used by the Internal Revenue Service or the Labor Department only in extreme cases of conflict of interests. The Service has indicated that it will particularly scrutinize situations in which loans are being used to purchase stock from controlling shareholders. Such corporate bailouts are discussed below.

Use of Plan to Purchase Existing Shareholder's Stock

Closely held corporations may want to use an ESOP to purchase employer stock owned by controlling shareholders or their estates. Due to the attribution rules the redemption of a shareholder's stock

---

[1]In a recent action, the Labor Department claimed that trustees violated fiduciary duties by buying $1 million in employer debentures without seeking an independent valuation.

by the corporation may be taxed as a dividend rather than being treated as a capital gain. Since there is no attribution of stock owned by a qualified retirement plan trust, an ESOP can be used to provide a market for a shareholder's stock without the threat of dividend treatment.

Originally, the Service took the position that the use of an ESOP, and particularly an exempt loan, in this manner might still lead to dividend treatment, on the rather tenuous theory that there was an indirect redemption by the corporation through a loan guarantee or other efforts to facilitate the ESOP purchase. The Service will now rule that there is no dividend if the following three requirements are met:

1. The combined beneficial interest in the ESOP of the selling shareholder and his spouse, parents, grandparents, children, and grandchildren does not exceed 20 percent, either of compensation on the basis of which contributions are allocated or in terms of account balances. Since an estate or trust is apparently not a related party for purposes of computing the 20 percent, a participant's stock could be purchased under this test from his estate so long as his estate was not his beneficiary under the plan.

2. Stock held and distributed by the ESOP is not subject to any disposition restrictions greater than those applying to a majority of the employer stock held by the stockholders.

3. The employer has no plan, intention, or understanding to redeem any stock from the ESOP.

There are other restrictions that apply to a purchase of a 10 percent or more shareholder's stock by an ESOP. The fiduciary responsibility rules discussed earlier may prevent a redemption. These include consideration of exclusive benefit for employees, the primary purpose requirement for exempt loans, and the prudent man test. Although any ESOP can purchase the shareholder's stock for cash if these tests are met, only a LESOP may buy such stock on an installment basis or arrange a loan guaranteed by the employee to finance the purchase.

In addition, a LESOP cannot be obligated to purchase stock on the occurrence of an indefinite event such as a shareholder's death. Thus, a LESOP cannot be used to fund a shareholder buy-and-sell arrangement until the shareholder actually dies.

OTHER LEVERAGING PROBLEMS

In addition to fiduciary responsibility, there are a number of other legal problems that arise when an ESOP is used to borrow money, or as a financing device for the employer.

Contribution Limitations

An ESOP, like any other qualified plan, is subject to a limitation on contributions of both a dollar amount ($32,700 in 1979) per employee, and a percentage of compensation (25 percent). Certain LESOPS and TRASOPS are subject to a dollar amount twice as high. This higher limit is often not available to small closely held corporations since it does not apply if more than one-third of employer contributions for the year are allocated to officers and more than 10 percent shareholders.

Obviously, any exempt loan must be amortizable within the contribution limitations. Otherwise the employer will not get a deduction for the excess contribution necessary to pay the loan. The plan may also be disqualified if it accepts the excess contribution. The employer may have to perform on its guarantee if covered compensation does not remain sufficient to amortize an exempt loan. One way to increase the amount of the loan that may be amortized within the limitations is to have the loan made directly to the employer, rather than through the ESOP. When this is done, contributions must only be large enough to shelter the repayment of loan principal rather than to amortize both principal and interest.

Permanent Plan Requirement

All qualified retirement plans, including ESOPs (with the exception of TRASOPs), must be intended to be permanent. In money purchase pension plans, annual contributions must be made in accordance with the plan contribution formula. Even though profit-sharing and stock bonus plan contributions are discretionary with the employer, substantial and recurring contributions are required for such plans. In a LESOP, the loan terms may be relevant to whether the plan is intended to be permanent. If the loan repayment can be deferred, or if there is a final balloon payment, the Service might contend that the plan is not intended to have substantial and recurring contributions.

Despite the permanency requirement, the employer may reserve the right to terminate an ESOP. An ESOP may be deemed terminated if the employer discontinues contributions for a significant period of time, due to business necessity. On termination all participants become fully vested. If the termination occurs for other than business necessity, within a few years after the plan is adopted, the ESOP may be deemed disqualified, retroactive to its inception. All prior contributions would become nondeductible. In addition, employees could be held to have received constructively any shares allocated when they obtained a vested interest in such shares. Moreover, business necessity may be harder to show in an ESOP, since only a contribution of the employer's own stock is required.

In summary, an ESOP should not be used as a merely temporary financing device. It must be viewed as a permanent employee benefit.

DILUTION OF CONTROL

The use of an ESOP can have only two results. Either the existing shareholders are diluted in both the long run and the short run, or the employer repurchases its shares and terminates the tax deferral. The cost of sustaining the tax advantages of an ESOP to the employer is dilution of its existing shareholders.

Dilution is primarily a practical rather than a legal problem with ESOPs. There are, however, various legal implications in the amount, type, and timing of dilution. Dilution has two facets—dilution of ownership and dilution of control. Very little can be done to prevent dilution of ownership, other than repurchasing stock. However, various methods of avoiding effective dilution of control are available.

Types of Employer Securities

A nonleveraged ESOP may invest in virtually any type of employer security, including preferred stock, nonvoting common stock, and debentures. The use of nonvoting common would permit the ESOP participants to share in equity growth without having a voice in the management of the corporation. The use of nonvoting preferred, or nonconvertible debt instruments, would limit participants to a fixed return or the possibility of a fixed return. These options are not open to LESOPs or TRASOPs.

Pass Through of Voting and Other Rights

Even if voting stock is used, dilution of control may be limited if the ESOP trustees, rather than the participants, vote the employer stock owned by the ESOP. Since the employer normally names the trustees, who are often the officers, directors, or controlling shareholders, the trustees will normally have interests identical to those of the management of closely held corporations. However, they are still fiduciaries and may be liable for voting the stock against the clear interests of the ESOP participants. For example, dividends may be in the interest of ESOP participants, whereas the controlling shareholders may prefer higher salaries.

In nonleveraged ESOPs of closely held corporations there is a requirement for the pass through of voting rights to participants for stock acquired after 1980. But these rights must only be passed through on corporate matters requiring (by law or the corporate charter or by-laws) approval of a majority of the outstanding common stock voted. The participants thus need not be given any direct voice in day-to-day management.

TRASOPs and, for stock acquired after 1978, LESOPS, must pass through voting rights even if the employer has publicly traded securities. Full voting rights still must only be passed through in registered or registerable securities. In addition, voting rights must only be passed through on stock allocated to a participant's account. Leveraged stock is allocated to a participant in a LESOP only as the loan is paid. Thus, it may be years before a significant amount of the stock purchased with an exempt loan is subject even to the limited voting rights requirement. Dilution of control may be limited in such cases.

Allocation of Stock to Controlling Shareholders

In a closely held corporation, the controlling shareholders and their family members are often employees eligible to participate in the ESOP. Thus some of the ESOP shares may be allocated to them.

To the extent that this is true, their dilution is reduced. However, there may be problems when one shareholder is an employee who participates in an ESOP and another shareholder is not employed by the corporation. The nonemployee shareholders will obviously suffer a greater dilution.

There are limits on how much stock can be allocated to share-holders employees. No employee benefit plan can discriminate in favor of officers, shareholders, or highly compensated employees. Thus, employer stock in all ESOPs must generally be allocated in proportion to compensation. The dollar value of the stock that can be allocated to an employee in any given year is limited to a sum that rises with inflation. These dollar limitations are doubled for LESOPs and TRASOPs, under conditions described in Section 1.

Vesting

TRASOPs require immediate full vesting. Other ESOPs are subject to the same vesting rules as any qualified retirement plan. Thus, participants' accounts must only be vested on attainment of the normal retirement age specified in the plan (or age 65 if earlier). Participants who terminate employment before normal retirement age must only be vested according to one of the four deferred vesting schedules provided for in ERISA (unless the schedule would discriminate in favor of officers, shareholders, or highly compensated employees).

In any case, full vesting cannot be required by the Service for less than 11 years of service. Thus, many terminating employees will only be partially vested or not vested at all. Moreover, if a participant dies prior to normal retirement age, 100 percent of his account may be forfeited regardless of any graduated provisions in the plan. If distribution to terminated participants is deferred to age 65, rather than being made on termination of employment, many fully or partially vested participants will not receive a distribution because they will die prior to age 65.

Since the nonvested portion of a participant's account is for-feited and reallocated to remaining participants on the basis of compensation, strict vesting requirements may mean that less stock will be distributed, and that shareholder-employees of closely held corporations will be allocated more. Thus, vesting requirements may greatly decrease long-range dilution. They may also defer the need for cash to repurchase shares.

Deferred Distribution Date

Legally, an ESOP is not required to distribute until the latest of the following occurs:

1. The participant attains age 65 or the normal retirement age stated in the ESOP (if earlier);
2. Ten years from the time participation commenced;
3. Termination of employment.

Distribution to participants terminating employment may generally be deferred until age 65. As noted above, this provision may also create forfeitures if it is coupled with a provision for forfeiture on death prior to normal retirement age.

Deferred Method of Distribution

An ESOP, like any qualified retirement plan, may provide for payments in installments or in the form of an annuity. There are only two limitations. One is that the present value of the payments to be made to the participant during his expected lifetime must be more than 50 percent of the present value of the total amount to be paid. The joint and survivor annuity rules must also be complied with if the plan authorizes payment in the form of a life (as opposed to a term-certain) annuity.

Distribution of Other Than Employer Stock

Only stock bonus plans must distribute employer securities. LESOPs, TRASOPs, and nonleveraged ESOPS other than stock bonus plans may distribute other assets. However, LESOPs and TRASOPs must still distribute employer stock if the participant requests it. In such plans the employer cannot assure that cash will be distributed. This is the most likely result, however, when the participant's choice is cash or an unmarketable minority interest in a closely held corporation.

Termination of ESOP

On termination, all participants become vested. There can be no more forfeitures, except possibly on death prior to normal retirement age. If an immediate distribution is made, the employer may be faced with a need for a large amount of cash to repurchase shares on an after-tax basis.

An alternative is freezing the terminating ESOP. When a plan is frozen, the trust continues, even though no new contributions are made and distributions are made only on the same basis as if the plan had continued. Thus, distributions will be postponed until participants die, retire, terminate employment, or reach normal retirement age. This may offer a much more manageable cash flow for the employer. In addition, it is arguable that when an ESOP is frozen, it is no longer an ESOP. The requirement to invest primarily in employer stock and to distribute employer stock may disappear. If so, however, an exempt loan may become a prohibited transaction unless the employer can get an exemption.

SECURITIES LAW PROBLEMS

ESOPs raise securities problems both because they invest in employer securities and because in certain limited situations the interest of the participant in the plan itself might be deemed a security. The application of the federal securities acts to ESOPs is unclear in many contexts. The problem areas are discussed below. State securities laws may also pose a problem. Since these laws differ for each state, however, it is impossible to treat them here. Employers considering adopting ESOPs should check with their attorneys to determine whether there will be any local securities conflicts or necessary filings.

Interests in ESOPs

The Supreme Court has held that interests of participants in noncontributory, compulsory pension plans are not securities and that the federal securities acts do not apply to interests of participants in such plans. This rule should apply to most ESOPs. The status as securities of interests in ESOPs allowing voluntary employee contributions (such as the contributory TRASOPs discussed in Section 1) is unclear. If such interests are securities, registration with the Securities and Exchange Commission (SEC) may be required unless the ESOP trustee is a bank or some other registration exemption applies. Moreover, the antifraud remedies of the securities acts would apply even if a registration exemption were available. Thus contributory ESOPs should be avoided.

ESOP's Acquisition of Stock

The current SEC position appears to be that an employer's contribution of stock to an ESOP is not a sale covered by the securities acts. Thus, no registration is required. If the ESOP purchases the stock from the employer, registration is required unless an exemption applies. Generally, however, either the private offering exemption or the intrastate exemption would arguably apply. Since this is unclear, the securities laws provide another reason for contributing stock rather than cash. A purchase from a distributee will generally be exempt because the distributee will not be an issuer (unless an officer, director, or major shareholder is involved). If the stock is purchased from an officer, director, or major shareholder, the private offering or intrastate exemption may be available.

ESOP's Distribution of Stock

The current SEC position appears to be that distribution of stock to participants or their beneficiaries does not constitute a sale under the securities acts unless the stock was purchased with employee contributions or the employee had the right to elect cash rather than stock. As discussed above, registration of the employee's interest in the plan may be necessary if employee contributions are permitted. If there is an exemption from such registration for the plan interest, it is likely to apply also to the distribution of stock acquired with employee contributions. Because of the SEC position on cash elections, ESOPs should be written so that the trustee, or plan administrator, elects the method of distribution.

Transfer of Distributed Shares by Participants

The current SEC position appears to be that employer stock distributed to a participant constitutes a restricted security unless the number of shares held by the ESOP and the number allocated to each participant are both so small in relationship to the total number of shares outstanding that the market impact of the shares is likely to be negligible. If the stock is a restricted security, the manner and timing of any subsequent disposition may be limited. The stock should contain a legend indicating these restrictions, and closely held employers should require the distributee to sign an investment letter. The distributee may always, however, resell the stock to the ESOP; this sale would be exempt as a nonissuer transaction.

Effect on Employer Under 1934 Act

An employer must file a registration statement and meet the reporting requirements of the Securities and Exchange Act of 1934 when it has $1 million in assets and 500 or more shareholders of record. In determining the number of shareholders for this purpose, the current SEC position is that stock held by the ESOP will be treated as held by one shareholder. However, when the stock is distributed by the ESOP, each distributee will count as an additional shareholder. Thus, it is possible (although not likely) that the use of an ESOP could cause a closely held employer to become subject to the very costly reporting requirements of the 1934 Act.

6

Valuation of Common Stock in ESOP Transactions

M. Mark Lee

THE terms "fair market value" and "adequate consideration" are used extensively in the law and regulations governing ESOPs, leveraged ESOPs, and TRASOPs. These terms refer to the price that must be placed on an employer's securities when: (1) a party in interest sells, buys, or conveys stock to an ESOP; (2) a put right is exercised; or (3) a right of first refusal is exercised.

Failure to use a price reflecting "fair market value" or "adequate consideration" can lead to serious problems and penalties. In addition to the prohibited transaction problems discussed in Section 5, tax deductions can be voided, and the Internal Revenue Service, the Department of Labor, employees, and stockholders can all start lawsuits.

Deciding at what price to purchase, sell, or convey an employer's security to or from an ESOP is the responsibility of the plan's trustees and the other parties to the transaction. The parties must act in good faith, and the price must reflect the fact that an ESOP (or TRASOP) exists primarily for the benefit of the employee participants and their beneficiaries.

In the case of an actively traded security, the "fair market value" is usually the price prevailing for the security in the marketplace at the time of the transaction. In the case of an inactively traded security or a closely held security (that is, a security issued by a private corporation), this "fair market value" must be established. Using an outside valuation expert is evidence of good faith in determining the price for ESOP and TRASOP transactions that do not involve a party in interest. If such a party is involved, the use of an outside expert is highly recommended by the Internal Revenue Service and the Department of Labor, although the price the expert places on the securities is not interpreted as binding by these government units. Thus, both parties in interest and the ESOP's trustee (who can be held liable) should understand the concept of fair market value and the valuation process.

REVENUE RULING 59-60

No formal guidelines for valuation have as yet been issued, either by the Department of Labor or the Internal Revenue Service, for inactively traded or closely held securities in ESOP and TRASOP transactions. Nevertheless, it is clear that both are currently using and intend to continue to use the framework for valuation laid out in Revenue Ruling 59-60 issued by the Internal Revenue Service. The original purpose of this revenue ruling was to outline and review in general the approach, methods, and factors to be considered in valuing shares of capital stock of closely held corporations for estate and gift tax purposes. These methods are also applied by the Internal Revenue Service to the valuation of corporate stocks that are inactively traded and the prices of which therefore may not reflect fair market value. The ruling was modified by Revenue Ruling 65-193 (1965-2 CB370) and Revenue Ruling 77-287 (IRB 1977-33).

Revenue Ruling 59-60 defines fair market value as "the price at which property could change hands between a willing buyer and a willing seller when the former is not under any compulsion to buy and the latter is not under any compulsion to sell, both parties having reasonable knowledge of the relevant facts." Court decisions often state that in addition, the hypothetical buyer and seller are assumed to be able, as well as willing, to trade and to be well informed about the property and the market for such property.

This definition of fair market value has implicitly been adopted by the federal government and valuation experts for ESOP and TRASOP purposes. The definition is transaction oriented. All factors bearing on fair market value in a particular instance are to be taken into consideration. However, fair market value is not book value—that is, common stockholders' equity based on the historical cost of the corporation's assets less its recorded liabilities. Book value is only rarely equal to fair market value.

The ruling lists eight factors, to be considered in turn, that a buyer or seller of common stock would consider fundamental, requiring careful analysis in all valuations:

(a) The nature of the business and the history of the enterprise from its inception.
(b) The economic outlook in general and the condition and outlook of a specific industry in particular.
(c) The book value of the stock and financial condition of the business.
(d) The earning capacity of the company.
(e) The dividend-paying capacity.
(f) Whether or not the enterprise has goodwill or other intangible value.
(g) Sales of the stock and the size of the block to be valued.
(h) The market price of the stocks of corporations engaged in the same or a similar line of business having their stocks actively traded in a free and open market, either on an exchange or over-the-counter.

The history of the enterprise is analyzed to determine the degree of risk in the business. A valuator should consider the corporation's past stability, its growth, and the diversity of its operations. Other facts are reviewed including, but not limited to, the nature of the corporation's business, its products or services, operating and investment assets, capital structure, plant facilities, sales record, and management—all of which are considered as of the date of the appraisal, with due regard for recent significant changes. Events that are unlikely to recur are usually discounted, as they are of little relevance to the future of the company.

A sound appraisal must also consider current and prospective economic conditions as of the date of the appraisal, for both the national economy (or regional economy if the enterprise services a region) and the industry or industries in which the corporation competes. In this regard, it is important to know what economic and industry factors affect the corporation, and what the outlook is for these factors. Items reviewed include economic and demographic projections; inter- and intra-industry competition; the relative competitive position of the enterprise in its industry; the severity of price competition; and the life cycle of the company's products. Generally, both the corporation and its common stock are more valuable if the corporation has a strong industry position and the outlook for its products is favorable.

To analyze the financial condition of the business, an appraiser needs the balance sheets of the corporation, preferably in the form of comparative annual statements for two or more years immediately preceding the date of the appraisal, and its latest interim balance sheet. Any balance sheet items that are not self-explanatory should be clarified in detail, and with supporting schedules if the items are material. These statements usually will disclose to the appraiser the liquid position of the corporation, the book value of the principal classes of fixed assets of the corporation, the corporation's long-term debt structure, its capital structure, and the net worth associated with its different classes of capital stock. These balance sheets should be audited, or supplemented, so that the appraiser completely understands any contingent liabilities and off-balance-sheet liabilities and assets of the corporation.

A comparison of the company's balance sheets over several years may reveal such developments as the adquisition of additional production facilities or subsidiary companies, an improvement in financial position, and details of recapitalizations and other changes in the capital structure and liquidity of the corporation. In the valuation of majority or controlling interests—that is, valuations involving blocks of stock that transfer actual control over the assets and organization of a corporation—the balance sheets can be used to identify any assets not needed in the operation of the business, such as investments in securities and real estate. In these appraisals, the value of the excess assets can be added to the going-concern value of the enterprise, as these assets can safely be removed from the business without impairing its earnings.

The earnings capacity of the business, especially prospective earnings capacity, is an important factor in all valuations of commercial and industrial concerns. Most going concerns of these types are priced primarily on the basis of earnings. All information that may be helpful in determining future earnings should be considered. Recommended techniques for determining future earnings include the analysis of detailed audited income statements for at least five years prior to the valuation date, separating recurring from nonrecurring items, and analyzing profit margins to determine the safety of net income. Supplementary interim income statements covering the year to date prior to the valuation date, and covering a similar period for the prior year, should also be reviewed, along with the corporation's budgets and projections. Corporations with good growth trends and profit margins are more valuable than marginal operations.

For majority interest or controlling interest valuations earnings should be analyzed in light of the potential elimination of unprofitable lines of business, the reasonableness of officers' salaries, corporate overhead and other discretionary expenses, the possibility of increased earnings as a result of new management, and the possibility of synergistic increases in earnings. Adjusting for these variables will tend to increase the value of the corporation and its common stock. However, these adjustments should not be made in minority and noncontrolling interest valuations because the running of the corporation will not change. In noncontrolling valuations, unusually high management salaries and perquisites should not be added back to the earnings of the corporation unless they are going to be eliminated.

The previous dividend payments of a closely held corporation are often deemphasized in majority interest valuations on the theory that actual dividends paid are influenced at least as much by the income needs of majority stockholders (and their desire to avoid income taxes) as by the need of the business to retain earnings for corporate purposes. Controlling stockholders also can substitute salaries and bonuses for dividends, reducing both the net income and apparent dividend-paying capacity of the company. Thus, in these cases, it is appropriate to adjust the level of both net income and dividends, if warranted. However, in minority interest valuations involving ESOPs, neither the ESOP nor its participants may be able to influence the running of the corporation. Thus dividends actually paid may be an important consideration in determining fair market value.

Goodwill, patents, and other intangibles such as production and sales organizations and management may be the most valuable

73

assets of the enterprise. Their value is usually reflected in the earning capacity of the corporation.

Arm's-length transactions, as well as outside offers to purchase the company, may also be important in establishing fair market value. On the other hand, forced or distressed sales of stock, or sales that reflect other special circumstances, are not often useful. Isolated sales of small amounts of stock may be useful evidence of value, even though they do not control as the measure of value.

The size of the block of stock and its power are relevant factors. A block of stock can be: a majority or controlling block, that is, a block large enough to influence or control the corporation's operations and assets; a minority and noncontrolling interest block, which derives its value from the earnings, dividends, and asset value of the corporation as it is currently run; or a swing block, a minority and noncontrolling block large enough to give the acquirer of the block the power to become a majority or controlling stockholder.

Majority blocks of stock can often be worth as much as 40 or 50 percent more than equivalent, readily marketable minority blocks of common stock. This premium may be even greater in comparison with minority blocks of common stock of privately held corporations. It has been established in court cases and in private placement transactions that stock that cannot be sold to the general public because of lack of registration with the Securities and Exchange Commission is worth significantly less than equivalent freely marketable stock when both are minority interests. The discount for this lack of marketability has been 35 percent and more. ESOP transactions involving the transfer of control should be carefully structured, or a minority interest valuation may become appropriate.

Ruling 59-60 notes that in many instances when a stock is privately held (or is traded infrequently) the best measure of value may be found in the prices at which stocks of companies engaged in the same or a similar line of business are selling in a free and open market. A public corporation's assets, performance, risks, and prospects can be compared with those of the employer corporation. Generally, the more similar a comparative public corporation is to the employer being evaluated—in terms of product line, profitability, and risk—the more useful it is in establishing the fair market value of the employer's stock.

ADDITIONAL FACTORS TO CONSIDER IN ESOP VALUATIONS

Five additional factors not included in Revenue Ruling 59-60 should be analyzed in all ESOP valuations:

(i) The legal terms and conditions of the ESOP, including employees' and distributees' rights and restrictions in holding and selling employer securities.

(j) Expected impact of the ESOP transaction on the employer corporation, on the ESOP, on third-party guarantors, if any, and on the value of employer's securities to individual participants and distributees.

(k) History, nature, and operation of the ESOP.

(l) Financial condition of the ESOP.

(m) Marketability, independent of the operation of the ESOP, of the stock of the employer corporation.

The terms of the ESOP may have an important effect on the determination of fair market value. Thus, plan documents should be reviewed to determine such factors as employee coverage, permitted transactions, vesting and distribution requirements, and provisions for put rights and rights of first refusal. In addition, the matter of payment, timing, and payor of employee obligations may be important. The purpose of this analysis is to determine the potential obligations of the corporation, third-party guarantors, and the ESOP.

In analyzing the expected impact of an ESOP transaction on the corporation, the ESOP, and any third-party guarantors, an appraiser should consider the sources of any funds paid out by the employer, the ESOP, or third-party guarantors; the use of any funds received by the employer or the trust; and the provisions of any ESOP loan agreements. The purpose of this analysis is to determine the impact of the transaction both on the value of the shares involved and on the corporation as a whole. As indicated in Section 3, these two effects can differ.

The history, nature, and operation of the ESOP, and its financial condition, are reviewed to determine the plan's ability to meet its obligations. Thus, its balance sheets and income statements should be reviewed in the same manner as that used for the employer corporation, taking into account plan requirements and the impact of the transaction in question.

The possibility of the sale of the corporation, or its "going public," may be important if the ESOP has a put right. Both possibilities can eliminate the repurchase liability and increase the value of the corporation and its stock.

WEIGHT GIVEN TO THE DIFFERENT FACTORS

The valuation of closely held, or inactively traded, corporate stock involves the consideration of all relevant factors. Depending on the circumstances in each case, certain factors may carry more or less weight than others because of the nature of the company's business and the particular transaction. The importance of minority or majority blocks of stock has already been discussed. Other factors may be important in specific instances. For example, earnings may be the most important criterion of value in some cases, whereas assets will receive primary consideration in others. In general, an appraiser may accord primary consideration to earnings when valuing the stock of a company that sells products or services, and may accord primary consideration to assets when valuing the stock of an investment or holding company or of a company with low earning power.

Put rights, too, may be more important in some cases than in others. In general, a put right will reduce (and in some cases eliminate) the discount for lack of marketability usually associated with unregistered, minority interest blocks of common stock, and thus significantly increase their value. However, this increase in value is possible only if it appears that the corporation, the ESOP, a third-party guarantor, or all three can meet the repurchase obligation. In fact, in some cases a put right might actually reduce the value of a corporation and its common stock because of the inability of the corporation to meet its legal requirements.

As a rule, voting rights are not a significant factor in minority interest valuations. Generally minority blocks of stock, even with voting rights, have little power in the running of the corporation or in the disposition of its assets. Occasionally, however, voting rights may be important, as in potential "swing" block situations.

A right of first refusal is a requirement that a seller of a corporation's stock first offer the stock to the corporation (or to its other

76

current stockholders) for a period of time before offering it to an outside party. Generally, a right of first refusal will not affect the fair market value of employer securities significantly in ESOP transactions if the purchase price offered is at fair market value and if the offering period is reasonably short.

Because the determination of the fair market value is a question of fact, and depends on the circumstances of each case, no formula can be devised that will be generally applicable to all valuation situations. A formula or weighting process excludes the active consideration of other pertinent factors, and its results are correct only by chance.

CURRENT METHODOLOGY

Revenue Ruling 59-60 and the decisions of the Tax Court have led to the use of the comparative-company method of determining the value of closely held and inactively traded securities. This method should be used for ESOP valuations. Under this method the procedure is to:

1. Prepare a summary of the nature of the corporation and its environment. This summary should include a brief history of the company, a summary of its revenue-producing activities, noting its products and services, its methods of sales and channels of distribution, markets served, its methods of producing and obtaining goods for resale, any dependency on customers and suppliers, the corporation's assets and economic strength, and its economic and industry position.

2. Prepare a five-year summary of the corporation's income statements and balance sheets. This summary should include the calculation of the following ratios for a period of five years:

(a.) Profit margins on revenues—which show how much of a revenue dollar is available after various expenses have been paid.

(b.) Trend and variability in revenues and income—which show how the revenues and income of a corporation have changed over time under different operating and competitive conditions.

(c.) Capital structure ratios—which show the composition of

77

the corporation's liabilities and stockholders' equity, and the degree of leverage of the corporation, which can increase both the financial risk and the profits of earnings available for common stock.

(d.) Liquidity ratios—which show how adequate the corporation's operating capital and income are to meet the needs of its business cycle, and the interest, principal, and dividend commitments of its capital structure.

(e.) Return on total assets—which shows how well the corporation has been able to generate revenues and earn a profit in relation to the total investment in the corporation.

(f.) Return on common stock equity—generally the most important ratio, which shows how well the corporation has generated a profit on sales and used financial leverage to generate a profit on its common stock equity.

(g.) Dividend payout ratio—which shows how much of the earnings available to common stockholders was retained for reinvestment in the corporation and how much was paid out as dividends.

3. Select publicly held corporations from the *Directory of Companies Filing Reports With the Securities and Exchange Commission, Moody's Manuals,* and *Standard & Poor's Corporation Records* for comparison with the employer corporation.

4. Collect and summarize from the latter two sources, from a company's 10 K reports to the SEC and annual reports, and from industry and economic sources, the same data about the comparative companies as were compiled for the private company.

5. Analyze the market price of the public corporations' common stock relative to their performance and characteristics. Generally, this is done by constructing three sets of ratios: price/earnings ratios, dividend yields, and the relationship of market price to tangible book value per share.

6. Develop a market price for the private corporation's common stock based on its performance and characteristics in relation to those of the comparative companies.

7. Determine the premium for control, if any, in majority and controlling-interest valuations, or determine the discount for lack of marketability in minority interest valuations. The appraiser determines the premium for control by analyzing premiums paid over market price in cash-tender offers for public corporations and by

analyzing the value of the corporation's assets, earnings, and cash flow under new management. He or she determines the discount applicable for lack of marketability by estimating the potential private market available for the closely held stock and by analyzing prices paid and accepted for illiquid stock.

8. Determine the impact of the ESOP and the transaction, including potential dilution in earning power or assets, and the impact of such factors as rights of first refusal and put rights.

Often an appraiser or trustee will find wide differences of opinion as to the fair market value of a particular security. In resolving such differences, Revenue Rule 59-60 states that he or she should maintain a reasonable attitude in the recognition of the fact that valuation is not an exact science. A sound valuation will be based upon the relevant facts, but elements of common sense, informed judgment, and reasonableness must enter into the process of weighing those facts and determining their aggregate significance.